Baking

With

Stevia

Recipes for the Sweet Leaf

by Rita DePuydt

Published by Sun Coast Enterprises

COVER DESIGN
Joe Papagni
COVER PHOTOGRAPHY
Baking Photos by Rita DePuydt
Stevia Photo by Joseph G. Strauch, Jr.

ACKNOWLEDGMENTS

Producing this cookbook has been a fun, exciting, and very challenging experience. I would like to thank the following people who helped make this project a success. I really appreciate all their help.

A special thanks to my family and especially my parents, George and Mary DePuydt, for their tremendous support. And again, thanks to my Mom for sharing recipes and baking tips. A very big thanks to my brother, Ray, for the many hours of computer advice.

Thanks to my friends Lyn Duguid, Doug Davis, Heather Hewer, Lucy Colvin, Steven Hill, and Lisa Neulicht for their enduring and unwavering support.

I'm grateful to Evelyn Frament for her steady support, her taste testing, recipe sharing, and advice.

Thanks to Russ and Pat Baggerly, Erica McDaniel, Marge Walker, and my neighbor Marvin Wilson for all their taste testing, critiquing, computer assistance and support.

A special thank you to Connie Rutherford for the computer help and for proofreading the book. I'm very grateful to Patt McDaniel for the generous use of her computer. Thanks to Daphne Hallas for her generosity and faith in the book.

Thanks to Vivian Taylor of the Fresno Bee for sending the stevia photos. Thank you to Wendy Fletcher for the loan of her tableware and for sharing her beautiful flowers.

I'm especially grateful to Joe Papagni for his expertise and great-patience in designing the cover. I really appreciate the testing and editing work performed by Lisa Ashcroft from the Wisdom of the Ancients company. Thanks Lisa!

Dr. Julian Whitaker
Dr. Whitaker's Newsletter, **December 1994**

"Stevia...is not only non-toxic, but has several traditional medicinal uses. The Indian tribes of South America have used it as a digestive aid, and have also applied it topically for years to help wound healing. Recent clinical studies have shown it can increase glucose tolerance and decrease blood sugar levels. Of the two sweeteners (aspartame and stevia), stevia wins hands down for safety."

Dr. Daniel Mowrey
Director of the Mountainwest Institute of Herbal Sciences

"Few substances have ever yielded such consistently negative results in toxicity trials as have stevia. Almost every toxicity test imaginable has been performed on stevia extract (concentrate) or stevioside at one time or another. The results are always negative."

Robert C. Atkins, M.D.
From Dr. Atkin's *Health Revelations* Newsletter, April 1994

"Stevia has virtually no calories. It dissolves easily in water and mixes well with all other sweeteners...I use it myself in delicious homemade ice cream that is extremely low in carbohydrates."

❖ CONTENTS ❖

5 COOKIES AND BARS

6 PUDDINGS AND PIES

7 TOPPINGS AND SAUCES

8 FROZEN DESSERTS

9 RESOURCES

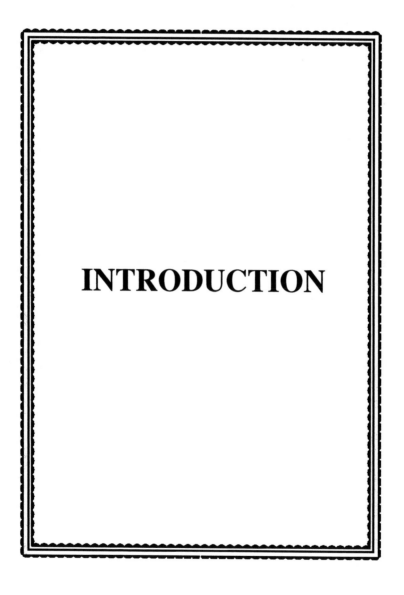

INTRODUCTION

Stevia rebaudiana

BAKING WITH STEVIA

The leaves of the South American shrub, *Stevia rebaudiana*, contain several molecular compounds that are extremely sweet tasting. Stevia extracts are estimated to be 200 to 300 times sweeter than sugar, yet stevia has no calories. These molecules are classified as glycosides; a number of which have been isolated to date, including stevioside and rebaudioside.

In addition to its sweetening capability, stevia is also considered a medicinal herb. This member of the Aster Family has been used by indigenous people in some Latin American countries for centuries. As a tonic, stevia reputedly stimulates mental alertness and counters fatigue, facilitates digestion and regulates the metabolism, and has a therapeutic effect on the liver, pancreas, and spleen. Stevia may actually help regulate blood sugar levels.

Numerous countries have discovered stevia in the past several decades. Japan, in particular, has done extensive research and safety testing on the plant. This testing has shown the herb and its extracts to be non-toxic, safe for diabetics, and beneficial in cases of obesity. In addition, stevia is not a source of nutrition for bacteria in the mouth and candida yeast in the colon.

In Japan, stevia is used commercially in prepared foods such as chewing gum, candy, soft drinks, juices, frozen desserts, low calorie foods, and baked goods. Stevia has garnered 50% of Japan's multimillion dollar market for high-intensity sweeteners.

With the average sugar consumption in the United States at 140 lbs. per person per year, this country would benefit greatly from a healthy natural substitute like stevia.

Stevia's flavor is not identical to sugar, but has a more "nectar-like" flavor. The sweet compounds are highly stable in heat and acids. The flavor is compatible with dairy products and acidic fruits such as strawberries, blueberries, oranges, lemons, limes, and pineapples.

Stevia is sold in the United States as a dietary supplement. It can be purchased in a powdered leaf form, as a white powdered extract, as a clear liquid extract, or as a green liquid concentrate.

A white powdered extract (without fillers) was used for all of the recipes in this cookbook.

While the powder and clear liquid extracts don't retain the medicinal properties of the whole herb mentioned earlier, they are a health boon to the American consumer by reducing sugar consumption. Research shows that the glycoside molecules are not metabolized by the human body and therefore pass right through.

About 1/3 to 1/2 teaspoon of the powdered extract has the sweetening capability of one cup of sugar. Sweetening potencies may vary slightly depending on the source. A liquid or a powdered extract may be used interchangeably in the following recipes. About 1/2 to 3/4 tsp. of liquid extract is equal to 1 cup of sugar. See page 92 to make a liquid extract from dried stevia leaf. The whole leaf, powdered and dried, may also be added to many recipes, such as breads and muffins, for added health benefits.

So little stevia is needed to sweeten a recipe, that adjustments were made to replace the bulk and characteristics of regular sweeteners. I relied on applesauce, apple butter, fruits, and nut butters.

Stevia greatly enhances a small amount of natural sweetener, such as fresh and dried fruit, fruit juice, maple syrup, and honey. The recipes in this book utilize this property. My goal was to keep carbohydrate-based sweeteners to a minimum, yet achieve superb taste, texture and appearance. I found that the addition of 1 to 2 tablespoons of honey, maple syrup, or date sugar greatly improved the flavor of some recipes, especially the cakes and pies. **You may wish to reduce the suggested sweeteners or eliminate them altogether**. In many of the recipes it will work, but a bit more stevia may be required. In contrast, if more carbohydrate-based sweetener is used, than less stevia would be needed. It's easy to add too much stevia, which overwhelms the taste buds. Use it judiciously.

For blender drinks, sauces, creams, and puddings, add the stevia in the beginning of the process. Adding it later may cause a thinning of the product. For muffins, breads, cookies, and cakes, I add the stevia to the liquid portion of the recipe.

Keep in mind that products made with stevia will not taste like those made with sugar. But quality, pleasant tasting goods can be produced. Bon Apetit!

Approximate Equivalents

1/3 to 1/2 tsp. powdered extract	= 1 cup sugar
1/2 to 3/4 tsp. liquid extract	= 1 cup sugar
1 1/2 –2 tbls. powdered leaf	= 1 cup sugar

INGREDIENTS GLOSSARY

AGAR-AGAR Flakes or bars derived from sea algae. Used as a gelling agent in place of animal gelatin. It supplies bulk and lubrication in the intestinal tract and increases peristaltic action, thus relieving constipation.

ALMONDS The fruit of a small tree related to the peach. High in protein, B vitamins, and the minerals: calcium, phosphorus, and iron. This healthful nut can be made into almond butter, almond milk, or ground into a meal.

APPLE BUTTER The pulp of apples, cooked, strained, and cooked further until thick and creamy. Several unsweetened brands are available.

ARROWROOT POWDER A starch from the tuberous roots of a tropical American plant used as a thickening agent in sauces and puddings. It is high in minerals and easily digested. Can be substituted for corn starch. Basic proportions are 1 tbls. of arrowroot to 1 cup of liquid.

BRAN The outer layers of grain. It absorbs moisture, providing bulk in the intestinal tract. Oat and wheat bran are most often used. Bran absorbs liquid in baked goods, as well, which may lead to a dry or crumbly product if too much is added.

BROWN RICE Whole, unpolished rice. Not separated from its bran and germ as white rice is.

BUTTERMILK Originally this was the residue from the butter churn. Today it is generally made from pasteurized skim milk with a culture added to produce a heavier consistency and to develop the flavor.

CAROB POWDER   Finely ground pod of the tamarind, also called St. John's Bread. An excellent bowel conditioner, it is also high in minerals, very alkaline, and rich in natural sugars. Used as an alternative to chocolate.

CASHEW   The cashew nut is the seed of the cashew apple, which grows on the outside of the fruit. A tropical American tree of the Sumac Family, cashews are a good source of vitamin D and B1 (thiamine), iron, protein, and unsaturated fats. This soft, versatile nut can be blended to a smooth white liquid that replaces dairy products as milk, cream, and whipped cream. It also can be processed into an excellent nut butter.

CORN STARCH A fine powder derived from the endosperm of the corn kernel. Used for thickening puddings and sauces. Causes digestive problems and allergic reactions in some people.

DATE SUGAR   Dehydrated and pulverized dates.

EGGS   Try buying eggs from free-running or cage-free chickens if possible. Chickens suffer tremendously on large commercial farms.

EGG REPLACER   A powdered form is available consisting of potato starch, tapioca flour, leavening, and vegetable gums. Also, tofu, nut butters, apple butter, and banana act as binders in a recipe.

FLOUR   Wheat flour's superb rising ability is due to its high gluten content. This quality has made wheat flour the norm for bakers. A number of other flours are available that may be used, in whole or in part, to add flavor and variety to baked goods. Some flours may produce a heavier dough and more leavening may be required. I recommend using whole grain flours as much as possible. Enriched white flours only replace several of the 20 or more nutrients removed with the germ in refining flour. Whole grain flours should be refrigerated to maintain freshness.

•**Barley** - Smooth, mild-flavored, and a very good substitute for wheat flour. Contains a small amount of gluten.

•**Corn** - Ground whole kernel corn, with a finer texture than corn meal.

•**Oat** - May buy oat flour or grind from toasted flakes (see page 15). Use in small amounts as a dry product may result.

•**Rice** - Finely ground rice. Has a gritty quality. See page 16.

•**Soy** - High in protein, it boosts the protein complement in food. Never eat uncooked because it contains an enzyme that blocks digestion. Toasted soy flour can be purchased. Soy flour is also 20% fat. It's strong flavor restricts use to no more than 25% of the total flour in a recipe. Soy flour provides a tender, moist, and nicely browned product.

•**Spelt** - A variety of hard wheat tolerated by those allergic to regular wheat flours.

•**Wheat** - Available in hard and soft varieties and further classified as spring or winter wheat, referring to the season in which they are planted. Hard wheats have a high gluten content that are best for baking bread. These are called *whole wheat*; with stone-ground whole wheat being the coarsest but retaining the most nutrients.

Soft wheats are ground into *pastry flour*. They are low in gluten and do not rise as well. However, they are finer and more suitable for baking. I recommend using *whole wheat pastry*.

Unbleached white flour is refined and enriched but has not been put through a bleaching process. It can be used when a lighter, finer texture is desired.

FRUITSOURCE   A brand-name granular or liquid sweetener derived from grapes and rice. Contains simple and complex carbohydrates and other nutrients. Granules were used in these recipes.

GELATIN   An animal by-product used for gelling.

HONEY   Produced by bees from the nectar of flowers. Nearly twice as sweet as sugar. Use moderately.

LEAVENINGS   Quick rising can be accomplished by using baking soda or baking powder. Baking soda (sodium bicarbonate) interacts with acidic ingredients like buttermilk, yogurt, fruit juices, vinegar, molasses and honey. Carbon dioxide bubbles are released that are locked into place by heat.

Baking powders contain both the alkaline and acidic components; usually sodium bicarbonate with either tartaric acid, calcium acid phosphate, or sodium aluminum sulfate. These compounds interact to form carbon dioxide. Tartaric acid powders are single acting with the action taking place in the cold batter. See page 15 for making your own baking powder.

Double-acting baking powders start work in the cold dough and have additional rising action in the heat of the oven. Phosphate powders are double acting, but most of their action takes place in the cold batter. Most of the action of aluminum powders takes place in a hot oven. They are more effective, but for health reasons, aluminum-free baking powders are recommended.

In recipes containing acid ingredients, both baking powder and baking soda are often used. A small amount of soda is needed to neutralize the acid and less baking powder is required.

Keep leavenings to a minimum; generally no more than 1 tsp. per cup of flour.

LECITHIN   Phosphatides extracted primarily from soybeans. Emulsifies cholesterol in the blood, breaks up fats into small particles, and regulates the deposit of fat in the liver. May be added to baked goods and other foods.

MAPLE FLAVORING   Concentrated natural flavoring in a glycerin base. Imitation flavoring not recommended.

MARGARINE   Some of the recipes call for butter or margarine. Most margarines are considered harmful to the health due to the presence of trans-fatty acids. Trans-free margarines are now appearing on the market. Some of these are hardened by the addition of palm or coconut oil. If you prefer margarine to butter, keep looking for the best choice.

MEAL   Coarsely ground grains, nuts and, seeds. Easier to digest than whole nuts.

OIL   Cold-pressed oils retain their nutrients. Safflower and canola oil are mild-flavored all-purpose oils containing over 90% poly-unsaturated fats. Corn oil is strong-flavored and heavy. Sunflower oil has a slightly sweet and buttery taste and contains about 60% polyunsaturated fats. Store oils (except olive oil) in the refrigerator to retain freshness.

PEANUT BUTTER   The seeds of a legume that ripen in a pod underground. Use unhydrogenated natural peanut butter for baking.

POPPYSEEDS   This seed comes from a different species than the opium poppy. Seeds may be roasted, steamed, or crushed to release more flavor.

RICE MILK   A naturally sweet, pleasant-tasting, and low-fat extraction of brown rice. In my experience, rice milk will not thicken with corn starch or arrowroot powder. It initially starts to thicken, then suddenly and completely loses it.

SEA SALT   Sea water which has been vacuum dried at low temperatures. Contains all the sea water minerals.

SESAME SEEDS   The seed of an herb that grows in India. Very high in magnesium, calcium, lecithin, and amino acids. Yields a flavorful oil high in unsaturated fats. Makes a nutritious milk suitable for children.

SESAME TAHINI   A butter made from ground white sesame seeds. It is 45% protein and 55% unsaturated oils. A nutritious and versatile substitute for a number of dairy products.

SUNFLOWER SEEDS A nutritious and economical substitute for nuts. Packed with magnesium, calcium, phosphorus, and unsaturated fats. Can be blended with nuts to make milk.

SOY MILK A beverage made from soybeans that can be substituted in equal parts for dairy milk. May be high in fat, so read the label. It works well in puddings. Can be purchased in convenient vacuum-packed carton with a long shelf-life.

TOFU A white curd made from soybeans and a coagulant in a process similar to cheese making. An inexpensive and versatile source of protein. It is measured by weight in the following recipes.

VANILLA An extract of the seed pod of a tropical American climbing orchid.

YOGURT Cow's milk cultured with bacteria that is beneficial to the intestinal tract. Also available from goat's milk and soy milk.

ZEST The colored, outer portion of oranges, tangerines, lemons and, limes. Contain high concentrations of flavorful oils. Avoid grating the bitter white layer underneath.

USEFUL EQUIPMENT

Basting Brush For applying butter and glazes to pie or bread crust.

Blender (Multi-speed) or Food Processor - Indispensable. I've had the same 10-speed Osterizer blender for nearly 20 years.

Hand Blender The high-speed Braun is useful for blender drinks, sauces, and dressings. Convenient and less clean-up time.

Cheese Cloth For separating liquid from pulp.

Colander For washing and draining fruits and vegetables.

Cookie Cutters

Cooling Racks To cool baked goods whether in the pan or out. Circulates air for faster cooling.

Cutting Boards Have a separate board for cutting fruit and working with bread or cookie batter. This will keep them from absorbing onion and garlic odors. If made from wood, the boards must be scoured periodically with lemon, baking soda, or bleach.

Graters 4-sided grater, wooden ginger grater.

Grater Brush A small wire brush. Makes a frustrating job easy.

Grinders Nut grinder, nutmeg grinder if you like to use fresh whole nutmeg.

Juicer Squeeze citrus by using a hand juicer or an electric one.

Measuring Cups and Spoons Graduated glass cups in 1 and 2 cup sizes, and larger if desired. Stainless steel or plastic nesting cup set. Two metal or plastic nesting measuring spoon sets.

Mixing Bowls Several large, medium, and small, but deep, bowls. Either glass, ceramic, or stainless steel. Lighter weight bowls are more practical.

Mixer Small electric hand mixers are helpful in making cakes, whipping eggs, and making frosting.

Oven Thermometer Oven temperatures may differ from the gauge. Some thermometers also are not accurate, but I prefer to use one.

Pastry Blender For cutting fat into flour.

Pastry Cloth and Cover for Rolling Pin Helpful in reducing the introduction of too much flour when rolling out refrigerator cookies and pie crusts.

Pot Holders Gloves or pads-nice thick ones.

Rolling Pin For rolling out pie crusts and cookie dough.

Sifter For thoroughly combining dry ingredients. Use a triple sifter. Never wash a sifter.

Spatulas Rubber spatulas for cleaning out the blender and the bowl. A straight-edge wooden spatula is good for stirring puddings.

Strainers A fine-mesh tea strainer for straining the pulp and seeds from citrus fruit. A hand-held 5-inch fine-mesh strainer.

Timer Never forget again!

Whisks For whipping eggs and combining liquid ingredients.

Wooden Spoons Solid and slotted.

BAKEWARE

The choice of baking pans makes a difference in the baking temperature, baking times, and the quality of the finished product.

Dark bakeware and glass absorb and hold more heat. Therefore, food cooked in such pans need to bake at a 10° to 25° lower temperature than food cooked in shiny metal pans which deflect heat. If the food is cooking too fast, it will brown quickly on the outside but not get done on the inside. When using dark bakeware, watch the item closely near the end of its baking time. Cover with aluminum foil if necessary.

In this book, the muffins, quick breads, bundt cakes, and double-layer cakes were baked in dark pans. The cookies, bars, and spring-form cakes were baked in shiny pans. The pies were baked in a shiny pan, except the apple and peach pies which were baked in a glass deep dish pan.

Heavier bakeware is better because it absorbs, retains, and distributes heat evenly. Light-weight cake pans and cookie sheets have dead or hot spots. You may double-pan a thin cake pan.

There is evidence that aluminum from non-anodized aluminum cookware dissolves into food and causes a whole range of health problems. Non-anodized aluminum cookware is banned in some countries. But in the U.S., it is widely used in homes, restaurants, and in the processed food industry. Choose an alternate material when possible. Below is a list of recommended bakeware.

2 round 8-inch cake pans
1 9-inch Tube or Bundt pan (8 or 10 inch)
1 8-inch Spring-form pan
1 9-inch Spring-form pan
1 8-inch square pan
1 5 x 9-inch cake pan
1 9 x 13-inch glass baking pan
2 loaf pans
2 muffin pans
2 cookie sheets
2 9-inch pie pans
1 9-inch glass deep dish pie pan

BAKING TIPS

Pre-heat Oven - It can take up to 20 minutes to get an oven up to temperature.

Measure Accurately - All measurements in this book are "level", unless otherwise noted. "Scant" denotes slightly less than the full amount. "Heaping" means a rounded mound above level. To "pack" an ingredient press down on the substance to get all the air out.

Preparation - It is generally advised that all ingredients be brought to room temperature before mixing. I start warming everything up, including the room, by turning on the oven and taking everything out of the refrigerator before I begin. On the other hand, avoid over-warming eggs and butter in hot weather.

Variables - There are a number of variables in baking including the size of the eggs, moisture content of foods, bakeware, oven proficiency, measuring and mixing technique, temperature of ingredients, and weather. At times, I can't get cashew or soy whipped cream to bind. It may be related to certain weather conditions.

Pan Size - Cake batter should fill the pan no less than half and no more than 2/3 full. If the pan is too large, the cake will not rise properly. If the pan is too small, the texture will be coarse and the batter may overflow or sink upon cooling. Loaf pans may be filled to 3/4 full. Fill muffin pans 3/4 full to full.

Oven Placement - If using two shelves, stagger the pans. Place oven racks where you want them while oven is cold. The usual position is on a rack slightly above center. Try placing on a rack just below center for cakes and quick breads that are browning too fast. A single pan should be placed in the middle of the oven. Two pans on the same shelf should have 2 inches between them and between all four walls of the oven.

High Altitude Baking - Adjustments to recipes may be required as the altitude increases. Adjustments vary depending on whether baking cakes, cookies, etc. and how high the altitude is. Some of the changes may include: under-beating the eggs, raising baking temperatures about 25°, and reducing the baking powder. See a standard cookbook for more details.

Overmixing of quick breads and muffins results in a coarse texture filled with holes and tunnels.

Testing Baking Powder - Place 1 tsp. of powder in 1/3 cup hot water. Use if it bubbles effervescently.

Making Baking Powder - Single-acting: sift together
> *2 tsp. cream of tartar*
> *1 tsp. baking soda*
> *2 tsp. corn starch or arrowroot powder*

Pie Crusts - Roll out crust between two sheets of wax paper or use pastry cloth and rolling pin cover. Chilled pie dough may handle better. To prevent soggy bottom crust, brush with egg white or melted butter. Brush top with milk for a golden brown crust, with cold water for a flaky top crust.

Refrigerator Cookies - The trick is preventing the incorporation of too much flour when rolling out the dough. A rolling pin cover and pastry cloth helps.

Blanching Almonds - Boil 1 cup of water or enough to cover nuts. Pour the boiling water over nuts in a bowl. Let sit 1 minute. Drain and slip off the skins with thumb and index finger.

Making Oat Flour - Spread oat flakes on a cookie sheet. Toast in 300° oven for 15-20 minutes until golden brown. Grind in a blender to a fine flour

Gelatin – If using gelatin instead of agar, soften gelatin in some of the cold liquid for a few minutes, then simmer until dissolved.

Making Sour Milk - Add 1 tbls. of fresh lemon juice or vinegar to 1 cup whole milk. Let stand for 10 minutes.

Rice Flour and Corn Meal - To eliminate grittiness, mix with the liquid in the recipe and heat to boiling while stirring.

Tofu - Can be purchased fresh or in vacuum-packed cartons that have a long shelf life. Don't use old, sour-smelling tofu for uncooked blender drinks or puddings. Fresh tofu can be stored in the refrigerator for about one week if kept covered with water in a tightly covered container. Change the water everyday for greater freshness. Sour-smelling tofu may still be used for cooking. Either shave off the outer portions or boil the cake in water for about 20 minutes. Tofu is measured by weight.

Eggs - Yolks add richness, moistness, and tenderness to baked goods. The whites act as a leavening. Eggs also bind the ingredients together. Fresh eggs are best, though 1 or 2-day old eggs may not beat to a proper volume.

Frozen Fruit - Frozen fruit, especially bananas, make blender drinks thick and creamy. To freeze bananas, peel first and place in air tight container or freezer bag. Bananas will turn brown after 10 to 14 days in the freezer.

Rancidity - Buy only fresh raw nuts and seeds. As with oils (except olive oil), store in the refrigerator. When fats spoil, they are said to be rancid. Oxygen, in the presence of heat and light, reacts with the unsaturated double bonds in the fat. This reaction produces peroxides; free-radicals that cause physiological damage. Oil, nuts, and whole grains, contain the natural antioxidants vitamin E and C. These are eventually used up in preventing fat decomposition. Rancid oils have a bitter taste. High frying temperatures of $400°F$ and above begin destroying unsaturated fatty acids. Smoking is a sign of oil going bad.

Storing Baked Goods - For longer-lasting freshness, store bakery made with whole foods in the refrigerator if not eaten right away.

SUBSTITUTIONS

1 tsp. baking powder = 1/2 tsp. baking soda +
                       1 tsp. cream of tartar

         or   1/2 tsp. baking soda +
                       1/2 cup buttermilk or yogurt

         or   1/2 tsp. baking soda +
                       1/2 cup molasses or honey

1 tsp. baking soda = 1/2 tsp. baking soda +
                       1 1/2 tsp. lemon juice

---

1 cup buttermilk = 1 cup cashew milk + 1 tbls. lemon juice
         or   1 cup yogurt
         or   1 cup sour milk
         or   4 oz. tofu + 1/2 cup soy milk +
                       1 tbls. lemon juice
Note: cashew milk is not a cultured product.

---

1 tbls. corn starch = 1 tbls. arrowroot powder
         or   2 tbls. wheat flour
         or   1 tbls. potato flour

---

1 egg (as a binder) = 1/4 cup cashew or almond butter
                       or tahini
         or   2 oz. tofu
         or   1/2 ripe banana
         or   packaged powdered egg replacer
         or   1/4 cup apple butter

---

1 tbls. gelatin = 2 tbls. agar flakes

MEASURES

1 tablespoon	=	3 teaspoons
2 tablespoons	=	1 ounce
4 tablespoons	=	1/4 cup or 2 ounces
5 1/3 tablespoons	=	1/3 cup or 2 2/3 ounces
8 tablespoons	=	1/2 cup or 4 ounces
16 tablespoons	=	1 cup or 8 ounces
1 pint	=	2 cups or 16 ounces
1 quart	=	2 pints or 32 ounces
1 gallon	=	4 quarts

tbl.
16 = 1 cup
32 = 2 cups
32 tbl = 96 tsp.

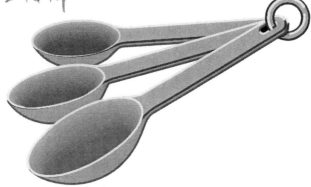

BEVERAGES

STRAWBERRY
PINA SMOOTHIE

3 cups pineapple juice
2 cups unsweetened strawberries (fresh or frozen)
1 banana (fresh or frozen)
1/4 tsp. stevia extract

Place all ingredients in a blender and process until smooth. Frozen fruit will make the drink thick and creamy.

Serves: 4

STRAWBERRY NOG

2 cups unsweetened strawberries (fresh or frozen)
1 1/2 cups of milk (dairy, soy, rice, or almond)
1 1/2 cups non-fat plain yogurt
1/3 tsp. stevia extract
2 crushed ice cubes (optional)

Process strawberries, milk, yogurt, and stevia in a blender until smooth. If the strawberries are not frozen, put crushed ice in the blender with the rest of the ingredients.

To crush cubes, place them in a closed plastic bag and hit them with a hammer.

Serves: 4

 # RASPBERRY CREAM

2 cups unsweetened raspberries (fresh or frozen)
1 cup milk (dairy, soy, rice, or almond)
1 tsp. vanilla
1/2 tsp. stevia extract
10 oz. silken tofu
2 tbls. oil (optional)

Combine raspberries and milk in a blender. Process until smooth. Add vanilla, stevia, tofu, and oil. Blend until creamy. Place in dessert glasses. Chill 1 hour or more.

Serves: 4

 # ORANGE COOLER

2 frozen bananas
juice of 2 oranges
1/2 cup yogurt
1/4 tsp. stevia extract (scant)
2-3 ice cubes crushed

Cut up banana and place in a blender with other ingredients. Blend until creamy.

To crush ice cubes place in a plastic bag, close, and hit with a hammer.

Serves: 2

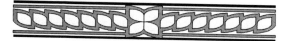

juice of 3-4 lemons (5-6 ounces)
purified water to make a quart
1/3 to 1/2 tsp. stevia extract (to taste)

Juice lemons and strain. If some or all of the pulp is desired then use it. Place in quart glass jar or other container and fill with water. Add stevia to taste. Chill in refrigerator. Stays fresh and pleasant tasting for several days.

Makes 1 quart

GINGER ALE

1/4 cup fresh ginger root (sliced)
1 lemon or lime (sliced)
4 cups water
1/3 to 1/2 tsp. stevia extract (to taste)
1 quart carbonated water

Peel and slice the ginger. Slice lemon or lime into 1/4 inch circles. Place ginger and citrus in the water in a pan and simmer for 20-30 minutes.

Strain the liquid into a glass jar or other container. Stir in stevia to taste and refrigerate.

To serve: pour equal amounts of the ginger/lemon water and chilled carbonated water in a glass.

Makes: 2 quarts

NOTE: **Simmer only! Do not bring to a boil because it will become bitter.**

OPTION: Add several stevia herbal tea bags during the last 10 to 15 minutes of simmering instead of, or in addition to, using the stevia extract.

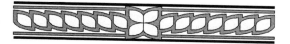

ALMOND AND CASHEW MILK

1/2 cup raw almonds (blanched) OR raw cashews
2 cups of water
1/8 tsp. stevia extract
1 tbls. oil
pinch of salt

To blanch almonds drop them into a pan of boiling water. Let set until water cools. Slip off skins with thumb and index finger.

Place either blanched almonds or cashews in a blender with part of the water. Pulse on grind. Add the rest of the water, stevia, oil, and salt. Blend until smooth.

Strain using a fine-mesh strainer. If cheesecloth is available, line strainer with it. Press out liquid. Pick up cloth and squeeze. If you don't have cheesecloth, strain twice.

Makes about 2 cups. Will store in the refrigerator for 4-5 days.

NOTE: Pulp may be used in baking, cooking, or as a bath scrub.

ALMOND MILKSHAKE

1 1/2 cups almond milk
2 frozen bananas
6-8 unsweetened strawberries (fresh or frozen)
1/8 tsp. stevia extract

To make almond milk, see page 26.

Cut up bananas and strawberries. Place in blender with rest of ingredients. Blend until creamy.

Serves: 2

HOT CAROB "COCOA"

1 quart of milk
4 level tbls. carob powder
1/2 tsp. stevia extract (to taste)
pinch of salt
1 tsp. vanilla
2 tbls. oil (optional)

Blend milk, carob, stevia, salt, and vanilla in a blender. Slowly blend in the oil through the top of the blender.

Pour into a pan and heat. Do not boil.

Serves: 4

NOTE: This beverage is rich and creamy made with almond or cashew milk. For a malt flavor add a tablespoon of Fruitsource.

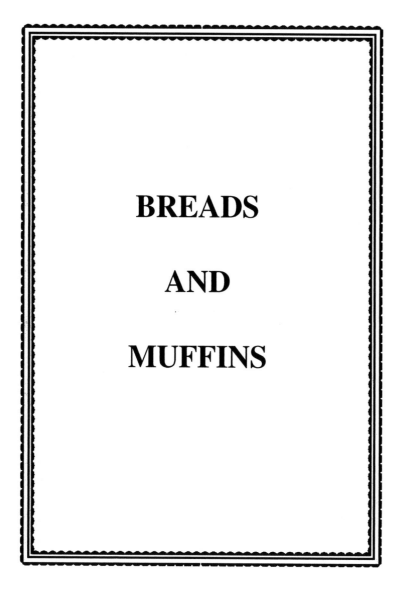

BREADS

AND

MUFFINS

APPLESAUCE GINGER BREAD

1/3 cup oil
1 large egg
1 cup unsweetened applesauce
2 tbls. date sugar
1/2 tsp. stevia extract
1 tsp. vanilla extract
1/4 tsp. maple flavoring

1 2/3 cups w.w. pastry flour
1 tsp. baking soda
1 tsp. powdered ginger
1/2 tsp. cinnamon
1/2 tsp. allspice
1/4 tsp. salt
1/3 cup chopped sunflower seeds (optional)

Preheat oven to 350° and oil an 8-inch square pan.

Beat the oil and egg together in a mixing bowl. Add the applesauce, date sugar, stevia, vanilla, and maple flavoring. Beat until smooth.

Sift the flour, baking soda, spices, and salt together. Fold the dry ingredients into the wet. Add sunflower seeds if desired. Minimize stirring.

Spoon into the pan. **Bake for 30 to 35 minutes**.

NOTE: A little more or less flour may be needed depending on how thick the applesauce is. Also more or less stevia may be needed depending on how sweet the applesauce is.

BANANA BREAD

1/2 cup oil
1/2 tsp. stevia extract
1 tsp. vanilla extract
1 egg (beaten)
1/2 cup plain yogurt or buttermilk
juice of 1/2 lemon
2 ripe bananas (medium-sized)

1 3/4 cups w.w. pastry flour
1/4 cup soy flour
1 tsp. baking powder
1/2 tsp. baking soda
1/8 tsp. salt
1/2 cups chopped walnuts (optional)

Preheat oven to 350°. Oil a medium-sized loaf pan.

Combine the oil, stevia, vanilla, and egg in a mixing bowl. Beat until creamy. Beat in the yogurt (or buttermilk) and the lemon juice. Mash bananas in a separate bowl then fold into the liquid mixture.

Sift the flours, baking powder, baking soda, and salt together. Fold dry ingredients into wet, stirring as little as possible. Mix in the walnuts before flour is completely blended.

Place into medium-sized oiled loaf pan (7 1/2 x 3 1/2 x 2 1/2). **Bake 50 min. to 1 hr**. until toothpick or fork comes out clean.

NOTE: For maximum flavor use very ripe bananas.

ZUCCHINI BREAD

2 cups grated zucchini (pressed)
1/3 cup oil
2 eggs (lightly beaten)
2 tbls. honey
1 tsp. stevia extract
1 tsp. vanilla extract
1/2 cup unsweetened applesauce
1/2 cup buttermilk

2 cups w.w. pastry flour
3/4 cup barley flour
1/4 cup soy flour
2 tsp. baking powder
1 tsp. baking soda
1/4 tsp. salt
1/4 tsp. cardamom
1/2 tsp. nutmeg
1 tsp. cinnamon
1/4 cup sunflower seeds (optional)

Preheat oven to 350°. Oil a large loaf pan.

Grate 4 cups zucchini. Zucchini contains a lot of water, and the larger they are the more water they hold. Remove the water by using a cheesecloth. Place about 1/2 cup of the grated zucchini at a time in the cloth and squeeze out the water. If you don't have a cheesecloth, squeeze with your hand. Four cups should be reduced to two. Put aside.

Beat oil and egg together in a mixing bowl. Whip in the honey, stevia, and vanilla. Add applesauce and buttermilk and beat. Fold in the zucchini.

Sift the flours, leavenings, salt, and spices together. Fold the flour mixture into the wet mixture, stirring as little as possible. Add the sunflower seeds before flour is completely blended.

Spoon into a large loaf pan and **bake for 55-65 minutes** until a fork or toothpick comes out clean.

NOTE: If you don't want to press the water out of the zucchini, reduce from 4 cups to about 3 cups. The liquids may also need to be reduced some.

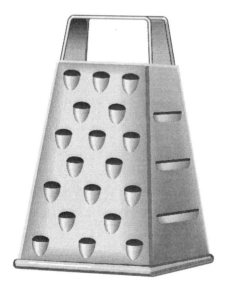

BLUEBERRY MUFFINS

6 ounces pineapple juice
3 tbls. oil
1 egg (beaten)
1/2 tsp. stevia extract
1 tsp. vanilla extract
1/2 cup plain yogurt
2 ounces milk
1 cup blueberries (fresh or frozen)

1/2 cup rolled oats
1 3/4 cups w.w. pastry flour
1 tsp. baking soda
1/2 tsp. baking powder
1/4 tsp. salt

Preheat oven to 375°. Oil muffin pans. Yield: 12 muffins.

Soak the oats in the pineapple juice for 10-15 minutes in a small bowl.

Beat together the oil, egg, stevia, and vanilla in a mixing bowl. Thin the yogurt with the milk and add to the other liquid ingredients. Beat. Mix in the soaked oats.

Sift together the flour, leavenings, and salt. Fold the dry ingredients into the wet, stirring as little as possible. Fold in the blueberries just before the flour is completely blended.

Spoon batter into muffin pans and **bake 25-30 minutes**.

SQUASH CORN MUFFINS

1/2 cup oil
2 eggs
3/4 tsp. stevia extract
1 tsp. maple flavoring
1 1/2 cups milk
1 cup cooked squash (packed)
2 cups w.w. pastry flour
2 cups corn flour
4 tsp. baking powder
1/2 tsp. salt

Preheat oven to 375°. Oil muffins pans. Yield: 18 muffins.

Whip together the oil, eggs, stevia, and maple flavoring. Add the milk and beat. Fold in the squash, just lightly mixing.

Sift together the flours, baking powder, and salt. Fold the dry ingredients into the wet without over-mixing.

Spoon into muffin pans. **Bake for 25 minutes**.

NOTE: Sweet squash like butternut or delicata works best.

OPTION: Add 1/2 cup fresh corn.

APPLE BRAN MUFFINS

1/4 cup chopped figs or raisins
1/3 cup unsweetened apple juice or water
3 tbls. oil
1 egg
1/2 tsp. stevia extract
1/2 tsp. maple flavoring
grated rind of 1/2 orange
5 ounces soft tofu
1/4 cup apple butter
juice of 1/2 orange

1 1/4 cups w.w. flour
3/4 cup bran (wheat or oat)
1 tsp. baking soda
1/2 tsp. baking powder
1/4 tsp. salt
1/4 tsp. nutmeg
1/2 cup chopped apple
1/4 cup chopped nuts or sunflower seeds

Preheat oven to 350°. Oil muffin pans. Yield: 12 muffins.

Simmer the figs or raisins in apple juice (or water) for 10-15 minutes.

Beat the oil and egg together in a mixing bowl. Add the stevia, maple flavoring, and orange rind.

Blend the tofu, apple butter, and orange juice in a blender. Add to the oil/egg mixture and beat. Mix in the stewed fruit.

Mix the flour, bran, leavenings, salt, and nutmeg together in a bowl. Fold the dry ingredients into the wet, stirring little. Fold in the chopped apples and nuts before the flour is completely blended.

Spoon batter into muffin pans. **Bake for 25-30 minutes**.

FRESH PEACH MUFFINS

1/2 cup oil
8 ounces silken or soft tofu
1 cup milk
2 tbls. lemon juice
1 tsp. stevia extract
1 tsp. vanilla extract
3-5 chopped peaches (2 1/2 cups- not packed)

3 1/2 cups w.w. pastry flour
2 tbls. soy flour
1/2 cup oat bran
2 1/2 tsp. baking powder
1 tsp. baking soda
1/4 tsp. salt
1 tsp. fresh ginger (grated)

Preheat oven to 375°. Oil muffins pans. Yield: 18 muffins.

Blend the oil, tofu, milk, lemon juice, stevia, vanilla, and 1 1/2 cups of the chopped peaches in a blender until smooth.

Stir the flours, bran, leavenings, and salt together in a large mixing bowl. Make a well in the dry ingredients and fold in the wet ingredients quickly and gently. Add the remaining chopped peaches and fresh ginger just before flour is completely blended.

Spoon batter into muffin pans to about 3/4 full. **Bake 25-35 minutes.**

"We will want to...reacquaint ourselves with the down-to-earth look and feel of cakes or cookies make from wholesome, wholefood ingredients. With the first bite, the more homey taste of this food will make sense to you. It will taste real. You will sense that it will do good in your body, and you will be perfectly happy that it will also look real!"

From: *The American Vegetarian Cookbook From the Fit for Life Kitchen*

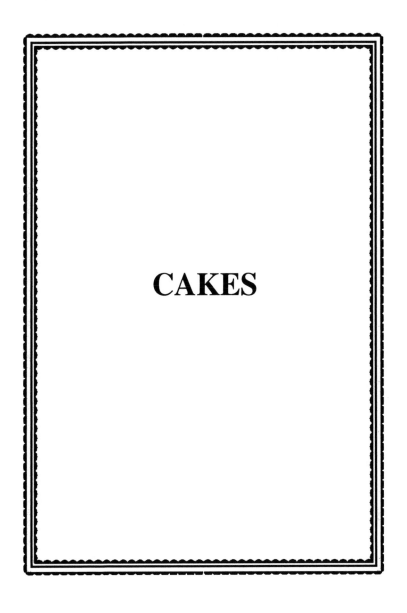

CAKES

STRAWBERRY CREAM CAKE

Double-Layer

2/3 cup oil
2 eggs
4 tbls. maple syrup or honey
1 tsp. stevia extract
2 tbls. Fruitsource or date sugar
2 tsp. vanilla extract
1 cup unsweetened applesauce
2 tbls. lemon juice
1 cup milk

2 cups w.w. pastry flour
1 cup unbleached flour
1/4 cup soy flour
2 tsp. baking soda
1 tsp. baking powder
1/4 tsp. salt

Place rack in lower third of oven. Preheat oven to 350°. Oil and flour two 8-inch round cake pans.

Beat the oil and eggs together in a large mixing bowl. Use a wire whisk or hand mixer. Beat in the maple syrup (or honey), stevia, Fruitsource (or date sugar). Add the vanilla, applesauce, and lemon juice. Beat in the milk.

Sift the flour, leavenings, and salt together twice. Fold the dry ingredients into the wet. Beat about 10 strokes with a spoon until batter is blended.

Divide the batter between the two pans. Smooth the top surfaces with a spatula. **Bake for 35-40 minutes**. Cool in the pans 10 minutes. Turn cakes onto a cooling rack.

If the center of the cakes peak, shave off one of the layers so it is flat.

Filling and Topping

2/3 cup Strawberry Filling
2 cups fresh strawberries
whipped cream

Put a generous layer of Strawberry Filling (pg. 79) between the cakes. Lay sliced fresh strawberries on top of the filling. Place second layer on. Serve the cake topped with whipped cream and whole berries.

BLUEBERRY TOFU BUNDT CAKE

2/3 cup oil
6 ounces tofu
1 tbls. tahini
1 tsp. stevia extract
2 tbls. date sugar
2 tbls. honey or maple syrup
1 tsp. vanilla extract
2 tbls. lemon juice
3/4 cup unsweetened applesauce
3/4 cup milk

2 cups w.w. pastry flour
1 cup unbleached white flour or barley flour
3 tbls. soy flour
1 tsp. baking powder
2 tsp. baking soda
1/4 tsp. salt
2/3 cup blueberries (fresh or frozen)

Preheat oven to 350°. Oil and dust with flour an 8-12 cup bundt pan. A smaller-sized pan (8 or 10 cup) would be best. Place rack in lower third of oven.

Mix the oil, tofu, tahini, stevia, date sugar, honey (or maple syrup), vanilla, lemon juice, and applesauce together in a blender until smooth. Blend in the milk.

Sift the flours, leavenings, and salt together twice and place in a large mixing bowl. Make a well in the dry ingredients and pour in the blender mix. Stir until well blended but do not overmix. Gently mix in the blueberries.

Spoon into the pan and smooth the top surface with a spatula. **Bake for 55-60 minutes**. Cool in the pan 10 minutes then turn onto a cooling rack. Top generously with warm Blueberry Sauce (pg. 78). Let sauce run down the sides of the cake.

CARROT CAKE

1/2 cup unsweetened coconut
6 ounces crushed pineapple with juice (8-ounce can)
1 tsp. stevia extract
2-3 tbls. Fruitsource or date sugar
1/2 cup butter or margarine (softened)
2 eggs (beaten)
1/3 cup yogurt
1/4 cup milk
1 tsp. vanilla extract
1/2 tsp. maple flavoring
1/2 cup chopped walnuts
2 cups grated carrots

1 cup w.w. pastry flour
1 cup unbleached white flour
2 tbls. soy flour
2 tsp. baking powder
1 tsp. baking soda
1 1/2 tsp. cinnamon
1/4 tsp. salt

Preheat oven to 350°. Oil an 8-inch spring-release pan or a 10 x 6 inch cake pan.

Soak the coconut in the pineapple and juice. Use all the juice from an 8-ounce can of pineapple but only 6 ounces of the pineapple. Set aside.

Soften and cream the butter (or margarine) in a large mixing bowl. Cream in the stevia and the Fruitsource (or date sugar). Gradually cream in the beaten eggs (they need to be at room temperature). Don't worry if the butter separates.

Thin the yogurt with the milk and add to the butter. Mix in the vanilla and maple flavoring. Stir in the walnuts, soaked coconut, pineapple, and carrots.

Sift the flours, leavenings, cinnamon, and salt together twice in a separate bowl.

Fold the sifted dry ingredients into the wet, stirring just until blended. Batter will be stiff.

Spoon batter into cake pan and **bake for 1 hour**. Cool in the pan.

Release the pan and top with Cream Cheese Frosting (page 82).

CHEESE CAKE

Crust

1 1/2 cups crumbs of graham crackers
or ginger snaps (finely ground)
6 tbls. butter or margarine (melted)

Place the crackers or cookies in a plastic bag, close the bag, and crush with a rolling pin. Place in a small bowl.

Melt the butter and mix into the crumbs until well blended. Press the crumbs into the bottom of a 9-inch spring-release pan. If preferred, crumbs may also be pressed 2 inches up the side of the pan. The crust may be baked in a 300° oven for 15 minutes or left unbaked. If used unbaked, the crust must be thoroughly chilled before filling.

Filling

4 cups of low-fat cottage cheese
2 tbls. butter or margarine (melted)
4 eggs
1/4 cup maple syrup
1 tsp. stevia extract
1 tsp. vanilla extract
1/4 tsp. salt
1/4 cup wheat flour
juice of one lemon
grated rind of one lemon

Press cottage cheese through a fine sieve (strainer). Blend melted butter into cottage cheese.

Beat eggs in a small bowl. Add eggs in 4 parts to the cottage cheese, beating well after each addition. Mix in the maple syrup, stevia, vanilla, salt, flour, lemon juice and rind. Stir until mixture is smooth and thoroughly blended.

Pour gently into cake pan. **Bake in 300° oven for 1 hour**. Shut oven off but leave cake inside the oven for 1 1/2 more hours. Do not open the oven door.

Chill the cake in the refrigerator before serving. Up to 12 hours is recommended.

Strawberry Topping
(Optional)

2 cups fresh strawberries
1/4 cup water
1 tsp. honey
1/8 tsp. stevia extract
1 tbls. cornstarch

Slice 1 1/2 cups of the berries in half lengthwise and arrange over top of cheesecake.

Crush the other 1/2 cup berries and place in a small sauce pan with 1/4 cup of water. Simmer for about 3 minutes and strain out the pulp.

Return the strawberry juice to the pan. Mix in the honey, stevia, and cornstarch and cook until it thickens.

Pour the glaze over the strawberries on top of the cheesecake.

POPPYSEED CAKE

1/3 cup poppyseeds
3/4 cup milk
1/2 cup oil
2 eggs
1 tbls. tahini
1 tsp. vanilla or almond extract
2 tbls. maple syrup or honey
1/2 cup unsweetened applesauce
1 tsp. stevia extract
1/4 cup lemon juice
grated rind of 1 lemon

1 1/2 cups w.w. pastry flour
1 cup unbleached white flour
1/4 cup soy flour
1 tsp. baking powder
1 1/2 tsp. baking soda
1/4 tsp. salt

Preheat oven to 350°. Oil and dust with flour an 8-12 cup bundt pan. A smaller-sized pan (8 or 10 cup) would be best. Place rack in lower third of oven.

Soak the poppyseeds in the milk. Set aside.

Beat the oil and eggs together in a large bowl. Mix in the tahini. Add the vanilla (or almond extract), honey, applesauce, and stevia. Beat with a hand mixer until batter is fluffy. Mix in the milk, poppyseeds, lemon juice and grated rind.

Sift the flours, leavenings, and salt together twice. Fold the dry ingredients into the wet just until well blended. Do not overmix. Spoon into the pan. Smooth top surface with a spatula. **Bake 45 to 50 minutes**. Cool in the pan 10 min. then turn onto a cooling rack.

Top with Lemon Icing (page 81) or use Cream Cheese Frosting (page 82) or Lemon Cream (page 83).

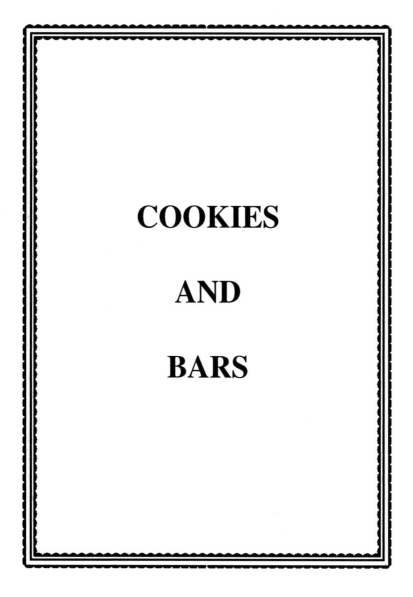

COOKIES

AND

BARS

CAROB CHIP COOKIES

1/2 cup butter or margarine (softened)
1/2 cup cashew butter
1/4 cup unsweetened applesauce
1 large egg
1/2 tsp. stevia extract
1 tsp. vanilla extract

1 cup w.w. pastry flour
1/2 tsp. baking soda
1/4 tsp. salt
1/2 cup carob chips (or chocolate)

Preheat oven to 375°. Oil a cookie sheet.
Yield: about 18 (2 1/2 inch) cookies.

Soften the butter (or margarine). Note: may use soft margarine in a tub. Cream the butter and cashew butter together. Blend in the applesauce. Beat in the egg. Mix in the stevia and vanilla.

Stir the flour, baking soda, and salt together; then mix into the liquid ingredients. Add the carob (or chocolate) chips and stir. Batter should be fairly stiff. Add a little more flour if necessary (one or two tablespoons).

Drop batter onto cookie sheet. Press down on the cookies once with your palm. **Bake for 12-15 minutes**.

1/2 cup raw almonds (finely ground)
3 ounces soft or regular tofu
3 ounces orange juice
1/3 cup almond butter
1/3 cup oil
2 tbls. date sugar or Fruitsource
1 tsp. almond extract
1/2 tsp. stevia extract
grated rind of 1 orange

1 cup w.w. pastry flour
1 tsp. baking powder
1/4 tsp. salt

Preheat oven to 375°. Oil a cookie sheet. Yield: 16 cookies.

Grind the almonds to a fine meal in the blender. Place in a bowl and set aside.

Blend the tofu and orange juice in the blender.

Cream the almond butter and oil together in a mixing bowl. Stir in the date sugar (or Fruitsource) almond extract, stevia, and grated orange rind. Add the blended tofu and mix well.

Stir the flour, almond meal, baking powder, and salt together in a bowl. Add the flour mixture to the wet ingredients. Add just enough flour so that the batter stops sticking to the sides of the bowl and forms a ball.

Roll dough into small balls with your hands and place on the cookie sheet. Flatten cookies to about a 1/4 inch thick with the palm of your hand. Press 1/2 almond, cut lengthwise, in the center of each cookie. **Bake 12-15 minutes**.

DATE NUT COOKIES

2 chopped dates
1/3 cup apple juice or water
1 cup ground walnuts
1/4 cup oil
1/2 tsp. stevia extract
1 tsp. vanilla extract
1/4 cup apple butter

3/4 cup w.w. pastry flour
1 tsp. cinnamon

Preheat oven to 350°. Oil cookie sheet.
Yield: 16 (1 1/2-inch) cookies.

Simmer the chopped dates in the juice (or water) for 10-15 minutes in a small pan.

Grind the walnuts in the blender to a coarse meal. Put in a bowl and set aside.

Coarsely grind the softened dates and the liquid in the blender.

Beat the oil, stevia, vanilla, and apple butter together in a mixing bowl. Add the liquefied dates and mix. Stir in the ground walnuts, flour, and cinnamon.

Drop onto a cookie sheet using two spoons. Make small dome-shaped cookies. **Bake for 15-20 minutes**.

NOTE: May use any combination of nuts and seeds instead of walnuts.

CASHEW COCONUT CHEWS

2/3 cup unsweetened coconut
6 ounces pineapple juice
1/2 cup raw cashews (coarsely ground)
1 tbls. tahini
2 tbls. maple syrup
1 tsp. vanilla extract
1/2 tsp. stevia extract
2/3 cup w.w. pastry flour (scant)

Preheat oven to 350°. Oil a cookie sheet.
Yield: 16 (1 1/2-inch) cookies.

Soak the coconut in the pineapple juice in a small bowl.

Grind the cashews in a blender. Set aside. Cream together the tahini, maple syrup, vanilla, and stevia in a mixing bowl. Stir in the soaked coconut and ground cashews. Mix in the flour.

Drop onto oiled cookie sheet using two spoons. Leave cookies dome-shaped. **Bake for about 25 minutes**.

OATMEAL RAISIN COOKIES

1/2 cup raisins (packed)
5 ounces apple juice
1/3 cup raw cashews or walnuts (coarsely ground)
1/4 cup soy flour
1/2 cup butter or margarine (softened)
3/4 tsp. stevia extract
1/2 tsp. maple flavoring
1 tsp. vanilla extract
1 large egg
1/4 cup milk

1 1/2 cups rolled oats
1 cup w.w. pastry flour
1 tsp. baking soda
1 tsp. cinnamon
1/4 tsp. salt

Preheat oven to 375°. Oil a cookie sheet.
Yield: 18 (3-inch) cookies.

Place the raisins and the apple juice in a small pan and simmer over low heat for 15 minutes.

Coarsely grind cashews in a blender. In a mixing bowl, cream the cashew meal and soy flour into the softened butter (or margarine). Stir in the stevia, maple flavoring, vanilla, and slightly beaten egg.

Cream 1/3 of the stewed raisins and all of the juice in a blender. Set the rest of the raisins aside. Stir the creamed raisins into the butter mixture. Add the milk and the oats.

Sift together the wheat flour, baking soda, cinnamon, and salt. Stir the flour into the other ingredients. Add the rest of the raisins. Don't overmix.

Drop onto oiled cookie sheet and flatten with the palm of the hand. **Bake 13-15 minutes**.

NOTE: Soft margarine may also be used.
  For reduced-fat cookies: substitute the 1/2 cup of butter in the recipe for 1/3 cup butter and 1/4 cup apple butter.
  If you don't want to add nuts increase the flour by 1/4 cup.

REFRIGERATOR CUTTER COOKIES

1/2 cup butter or margarine (softened)
2 eggs
3/4 tsp. stevia extract
1 tsp. vanilla extract
2 tbls. maple syrup
1/2 cup ground raw nuts
1 2/3 cups w.w. pastry flour (scant)
1 tsp. baking powder
1/8 tsp. salt

Yield: 20 (2 1/2-inch) cookies.

Soften and cream the butter (or margarine) in a mixing bowl. Cream the eggs into the butter. Eggs need to be at room temperature. Mix in the stevia, vanilla, and maple syrup.

Grind the nuts in a blender. Mix the flour, nut meal, baking soda, and salt together in a bowl. Stir the flour mixture into the butter mixture. Add flour until dough balls up and stops sticking to the sides of the bowl. Be careful not to add too much flour.

Refrigerate dough for at least 3-4 hours. Preheat oven to 375°. Oil a cookie sheet. Roll out dough on lightly floured board. Cut dough with cookie cutters. **Bake for 12 minutes**.

VARIATIONS: Add grated lemon peel + 1 tsp. lemon juice
OR: Add grated orange peel + 1/2 tsp. almond extract.

CRISSCROSS PEANUT BUTTER COOKIES

1/2 cup butter or margarine (softened)
2/3 cup peanut butter (natural)
1/2 tsp. stevia extract
2 tbls. granulated Fruitsource
1/2 tsp. maple flavoring
1/4 cup apple butter OR 1 egg

3/4 cup w.w. pastry flour
1/2 tsp. baking soda
1/2 tsp. cinnamon
1/8 tsp. salt

Preheat the oven to 350°. Oil a cookie sheet.
Yield: 16 large cookies.

Soften and cream the butter (or margarine) in a mixing bowl. Cream the peanut butter into the butter. Mix in the stevia, maple syrup, maple flavoring, and apple butte r (or egg). Beat until thick and creamy.

Stir the flour, baking soda, cinnamon, and salt together in a bowl. Add the flour mixture to the peanut butter mixture.

Place large balls of batter on the cookie sheet using two spoons. Flatten each cookie with a floured fork making a crisscross pattern.

Bake for 15 minutes.

FOR REDUCED FAT PEANUT BUTTER COOKIES USE:
1/4 cup butter, 1/2 cup peanut butter, 2 tbls. oil, 1/4 cup apple butter, 1 egg, 1/2 tsp. stevia extract, 2 tbls. Fruitsource, 1/2 tsp. maple flavoring, 1 cup w. w. pastry flour, 1/2 tsp. baking soda, 1/2 tsp. cinnamon, 1/8 tsp. salt.

CAROB BROWNIES

1/2 cup oil
4-5 ounces silken or soft tofu
3/4 cup unsweetened applesauce
1/2 tsp. stevia
1 tsp. vanilla extract
1 tbls. lemon juice
2/3 cup carob powder

1 1/4 cups w.w. pastry flour (scant)
1/4 cup soy flour
1 tsp. baking powder
1/2 tsp. baking soda
1/4 tsp. salt
1/2 cup chopped walnuts (optional)

Preheat the oven to 350°. Oil an 8-inch square pan.

Place the oil, tofu, applesauce, stevia, vanilla, and lemon juice into a blender. Blend until smooth and pour into a large mixing bowl. Stir in the carob powder until well blended.

Sift the flours, leavenings, and salt together. Fold the dry ingredients into the wet. Mix in the walnuts. Don't over mix. Spoon batter into pan. **Bake for 30 minutes**.

PUMPKIN BARS

2 small eggs + 1 tbls. milk OR
1 large egg + 2 tbls. milk
1/2 cup oil
1/2 tsp. stevia extract
1/2 tsp. maple flavoring
2 tbls. date sugar
1 cup cooked pumpkin or squash (packed)

1 1/4 cups w.w. pastry flour
1/4 cup soy flour
1 1/2 tsp. baking powder
1 tsp. cinnamon
1/4 tsp. cloves
1/4 tsp. nutmeg
1/8 tsp. salt
1/4 cup chopped sunflower seeds (optional)

Preheat oven to 350°. Oil an 8-inch square pan.

Lightly beat the eggs and milk in a small bowl. Beat the oil in a large mixing bowl with the stevia, maple flavoring, date sugar. Stir in the beaten egg. Gently mix in the pumpkin or squash.

Sift the flours, baking powder, spices, and salt together. Fold the dry ingredients into the wet. Add the sunflower seeds just before the flour is completely blended. Batter will be stiff.

Spoon the batter into the pan. **Bake for 30-35 minutes**.

1 tbl = 3 tsp.

75% less sugar than regular

CHOCOLATE BROWNIES

4 squares unsweetened Baker's chocolate
6 tbls. butter or margarine (softened)
1/2 cup low-fat cottage cheese
1/4 cup honey or maple syrup *28 g.*
2 tbls. date sugar or Fruitsource *22.5 g.*
1/4 cup apple butter *40 g.*
3/4 tsp. stevia extract
1 tsp. vanilla extract
2 eggs

1 cup w.w. pastry flour
1/2 tsp. baking soda
1/4 tsp. salt
1/2 cup chopped walnuts

90.5 grams

Preheat the oven to 350°. Oil an 8-inch square pan.

Melt the chocolate over low heat in a heavy-bottom pan or double boiler.

Soften and cream the butter (or margarine) in a mixing bowl. Stir in the melted chocolate.

Put the cottage cheese through a fine-meshed sieve, then mix into the butter and chocolate. Blend in the honey (or maple syrup) and the date sugar (or Fruitsource). Mix in the apple butter, stevia, and vanilla. Beat the eggs in one at a time.

Mix the flour, baking soda, and salt together. Stir the dry ingredients into the wet until blended. Mix in the walnuts.

Spoon the batter into the pan and **bake for 35-40 minutes**.

regular brownies
2 cups sugar = 384 sugar grams

293.50 grams less

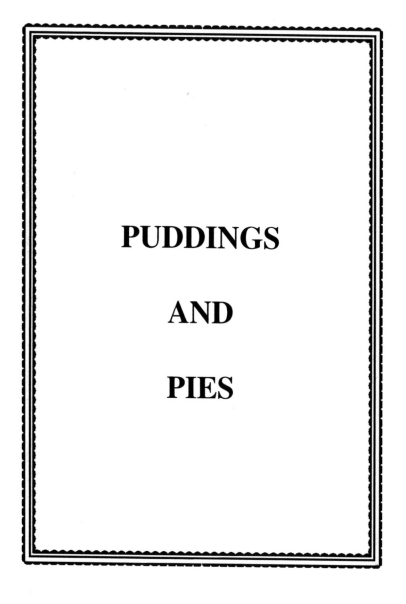

PUDDINGS

AND

PIES

SWEET POTATO RICE PUDDING

1/2 cup cooked sweet potato (packed)
1 2/3 cups milk
1/2 tsp. stevia extract
2 cups short-grain brown rice (cooked)
1 tsp. vanilla extract
1/4 tsp. cinnamon
dash of cardamom (optional)
pinch of salt

Blend the cooked sweet potato and the milk in a blender with the stevia. To cook the sweet potato: peel, cut into pieces, and steam.

Place the cooked rice in a medium-sized heavy bottom sauce pan. Pour the blended potato and milk into the pan. Cook over medium heat for about 15 minutes or until the pudding is thick. Add the vanilla, spices, salt, and stir. Cook a few minutes longer.

Serves: 4

NOTE: This pudding is excellent served warm with cashew cream.

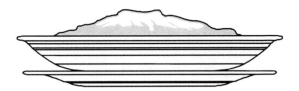

BANANA DATE PUDDING

4 chopped dates
1 pound soft or silken tofu
4 tbls. oil
1/2 tsp. stevia extract
1 1/2 tsp. vanilla extract
2 ripe bananas

Chop the dates and place in a blender. Add part of the tofu and oil. Grind. Add more tofu and oil along with the stevia, vanilla, and banana. Blend until creamy. Use the pulse button, stirring between pulses. Note: May use a food processor.

Spoon into dessert glasses or bowls. Chill 1-2 hours.

Serves: 4

VANILLA PUDDING

2 tbls. arrowroot powder or corn starch
2 tbls. w.w. pastry flour
1/2 tsp. stevia extract
pinch of salt
2 cups vanilla-flavored soy milk

Mix the arrowroot powder, flour, stevia, and salt together in a cup or small bowl. Make a paste with some of the milk. Gradually thin out the paste until it will pour. Eliminate any lumps.

Gently heat the rest of the milk on low heat. Slowly add the arrowroot/flour mixture, stirring gently with a wooden spatula or spoon. Simmer over low heat for 3-5 minutes. The mixture will thicken quickly if using arrowroot powder.

Spoon the pudding into dessert glasses or bowls.

Serves: 4

NOTES: If using plain soy milk, add 2 tsp. vanilla extract. I was unable to thicken rice milk.

If using corn starch as the thickener, cook the pudding on low heat for a total of 10 minutes to make sure the starch is cooked.

PUMPKIN PIE

Single 9-inch Crust

1/4 tsp. salt
1 cup w.w. pastry flour
2 tbls. soy flour
4 tbls. soft soy or canola margarine
3 tbls. cold water

Mix the salt into the flour. Cut the margarine into the flour with a pastry blender or fork until well distributed and looks like a coarse meal. Sprinkle the water in gradually while mixing the flour.

Form into a ball and roll out between two pieces of wax paper. Remove top sheet of paper and flip crust over into a pie pan. Remove other paper. Trim and flute edges.

Filling

10 to 12 ounces soft or silken tofu
1/3 cup oil
2 cups fresh cooked pumpkin (packed) OR
1 15-ounce can of plain pumpkin
2 tbls. maple syrup
1 tbls. Fruitsource or date sugar
1/2 tsp. maple flavoring
1/2 tsp. stevia extract
*1/4 tsp. salt * 1 tsp. cinnamon*
*1/2 tsp. ginger * 1/4 tsp. nutmeg*

Preheat oven to 350°.

Blend all the ingredients for the filling until smooth and creamy in a blender or food processor. If using a blender, start with some of the tofu and the oil. Gradually add the rest of the ingredients. Use the pulse button; stirring in between pulses.

Pour into an unbaked pie shell. **Bake for 1 hour**. Chill and serve topped with Whipped Cream (see page 84 or 85 or use dairy whipped cream).

BLACKBERRY CREAM PIE

Nut & Seed Crust
(9-inch pie shell)

1/2 cup chopped figs or raisins
1/2 cup chopped dates
2 tbls. apple juice or water
1/4 cup unsweetened coconut
1/2 cup raw sesame seeds
1/4 cup raw sunflower seeds
1/3 cup raw almonds

Toasting the crust is optional. Preheat oven to 300° if you wish to toast it first.

Place chopped fruit in a small sauce pan with the juice and soften over low heat for a few minutes.

Grind the nuts and seeds to a fine meal in a blender. Place in a bowl and mix in the fruit. Grind the mixture in the blender. Place about 1/3 of it at a time in the blender. Use the pulse button, stirring between pulses. When blended and ground, remove and put in another portion to grind. Note: may use a food processor.

Press the mixture into the bottom and sides of a 9-inch pie pan. Bake for 15 minutes if desired. If baked, cool before filling. If unbaked, chill in the refrigerator before filling.

NOTE: May use any combination of nuts, seeds, and fruit for the crust. May also use the Crumb Crust (pg. 46) or the Granola Crust (pg. 72) if preferred.

Filling

4 cups ripe blackberries (fresh or frozen)
1 cup of water
1 cup of unsweetened apple juice
2 tbls. lemon juice
pinch of salt
10 ounces soft or silken tofu
1 tsp. vanilla extract
3/4 tsp. stevia extract
3 tbls. agar-agar (or 1 1/2 pkgs. gelatin)

Cook the blackberries in the water, apple juice, lemon juice, and salt until the fruit is completely broken down. After cooking, press the berries through a fine-meshed strainer to remove the seeds. Will have 2 cups of hot berry sauce. If you have more, boil it down until you only have 2 cups.

NOTE: Frozen berries may be used but cut back on the cooking liquid from 2 cups to about 1 1/2 cups. As above, you need to end up with 2 cups of berry sauce.

Blend the tofu, vanilla, and stevia in a blender until creamy with one cup of the berry sauce.

Place the other cup of berry sauce in a small pan. Dissolve the agar-agar in the hot sauce. Bring to a boil and reduce to a simmer, cooking until dissolved (3-4 minutes), stirring occasionally.

Add the berry sauce with the dissolved agar-agar to the mixture in the blender and process until smooth and creamy.

Pour the blender contents into the cooled pie shell. Chill 1-2 hours.

OPTION: Serve topped with Whipped Cream. See page 84 or 85.

APPLE PIE

Quick and Easy Pie Crust
(2-crust)

1/4 tsp. salt
2 cups w.w. pastry flour
2 tbls. soy flour
1/2 cup oil
1/4 cup cold soy milk or water

Mix the salt into the flour. Pour the oil and milk (or water) into a cup without stirring. Mix into the flour with a fork or pastry blender. Form into a ball. Break into two with one part a bit larger than the other. Roll out bottom crust between two pieces of wax paper. Place in a 9-inch deep dish pie pan or other 9-inch pan.

NOTE: May use the margarine crust on page 65- double the recipe.

Filling

8-10 large ripe apples (should form a heaping
mound in the pie pan)
juice of 1/2 lemon
1/4 cup apple butter
2 tbls. arrowroot powder
2 tbls. w.w. flour
1 tsp. cinnamon
1/4 tsp. nutmeg
1 tsp. stevia extract
2-3 tbls. date sugar or Fruitsource
1/4 tsp. salt
2 tbls. butter or margarine

Preheat oven to 450°.

Peel (optional), core, and slice apples into a large bowl. Sprinkle lemon juice over apples and mix.

Stir the apple butter into the apples.

Mix the arrowroot powder, flour, spices, stevia, date sugar (or Fruitsource), and salt together in a small bowl. Stir the dry ingredients into the apples, coating every piece. Cut the butter or margarine into pieces and mix into the apples. Place apples in an uncooked pie shell.

Roll out the top crust between two pieces of wax paper. Cut in the steam holes and place over pie. Fold top crust edge under bottom crust edge and flute.

Bake at 450° for 10 minutes. Reduce temperature to 350° and bake for 35-40 minutes longer.

NOTE: If the apples are tart, may need more stevia.

LEMON MERINGUE PIE

Crust

Prepare a single 9-inch pie shell. See page 65 or 68 for recipes. Prick pie shell with a fork and **bake at 425° for 10-12 minutes**.

Filling

> *3 egg yolks*
> *juice of 2 lemons (3-4 ounces)*
> *finely grated rind of 2 lemons*
> *6 tbls. corn starch*
> *1 cup water*
> *1 1/2 cups soy or dairy milk*
> *3-4 tbls. honey or maple syrup*
> *1 tsp. stevia (scant)*
> *pinch of salt*

Reduce oven temperature to 350°.

Separate the yolks from the whites. Put aside. Save whites for the meringue.

Juice the lemons and grate the rind into a small bowl. Put aside.

Dissolve the corn starch in 1/2 cup of the water in a cup or small bowl. Heat the rest of the water and the milk in a heavy-bottomed sauce pan or double boiler. Stir in the honey (or maple syrup), stevia, and salt. When hot, but not boiling, slowly mix in the corn starch. Cook on low, stirring gently until thick (about 5 minutes). Simmer about 3-5 minutes longer on low.

Mix the egg yolks, lemon juice and rind together. Gradually mix about 1 cup of the hot pudding into the eggs. Add the mixture slowly back into the pan. Cook for 3-5 minutes longer on low, stirring gently.

Remove pudding from the heat. Cool to a warm temperature. To prevent a skin from forming place a piece of wax paper on the surface.

Place the filling in the pre-baked pie shell. Top with the meringue.

Meringue

3 egg whites
1/4 tsp. cream of tartar
1 tsp. honey
1/2 tsp. vanilla extract
pinch of stevia extract

Beat the egg whites until frothy at medium speed. Add the cream of tartar.

Whip on medium-high until whites form soft peaks that droop. Drizzle in the honey, then add the vanilla and stevia.

Continue beating on medium-high until the whites are smooth, moist, and shiny, and when the beater is lifted it stands in straight peaks.

Spread meringue on pie making sure it goes all the way to the edge. Form peaks with a knife if desired.

Bake in a 350° oven for 15 to 18 minutes. If the peaks are getting too dark, take the pie out of the oven early. Next time, try lowering the oven temperature slightly or lower the oven rack.

STRAWBERRY CREAM PIE

Granola Crust

1 1/3 cups granola
3 tbls. oil
2 tbls. apple juice or water

Preheat oven to 300°.

Grind the granola in a blender until fine. Place in a bowl and stir in the oil lightly with a fork. Sprinkle and stir in the juice (or water).

Press mixture into the bottom and sides of a 9-inch pie pan. Bake for 15 minutes. Chill before filling.

NOTE: May use the Crumb Crust recipe (pg. 46) or the Nut & Seed Crust recipe (pg. 66).

Filling

1 cup of whipped cream
4 cups fresh strawberries or 3 cups frozen (sliced)
2 tbls. date sugar
1/2 tsp. stevia extract
pinch of salt
1 banana
2 1/2 tbls. agar-agar (or 1 pkg. gelatin)
1/2 cup apple juice

Have ready 1 cup of whipped cream. Use whipped dairy cream or tofu whipped cream (page 85).

Slice the berries. Put aside 1 cup of the berries. Crush the rest of the berries in a bowl. Stir in the date sugar, stevia, and salt.

Put a layer of sliced strawberries in the bottom of the cooled pie shell. Put a layer of sliced bananas on top of the strawberries. Follow with another layer of strawberries.

Dissolve the agar-agar in the apple juice and simmer over medium heat for 3-4 minutes, stirring occasionally. Mix the dissolved agar-agar into the crushed berries.

Fold in a cup of whipped cream. Pour the filling into the pie pan. Chill for 1-2 hours.

NOTE: For a creamy filling, blend the 3 cups of sliced strawberries in the blender first. If using blended strawberries and tofu whipped cream, the entire filling can be made in the blender.

NOTE: If using frozen berries omit the layering in the bottom of the pie shell or layer with only the bananas. Thaw 3 cups of cut up frozen berries and blend in a blender with whipped cream. Use a total of 3 1/2 tbls. agar-agar.

PEACH CRUMBLE

Filling

8-10 fresh ripe peaches
1/2 tsp. stevia extract
2 tbls. Fruitsource or date sugar
1/4 cup unsweetened fruit juice
2 tbls. arrowroot powder
1 tsp. cinnamon
1 tsp. vanilla extract
pinch of salt

Preheat oven to 375°. Butter the bottom and sides of a 9 x 13-inch glass baking pan.

Peel and slice the peaches into a mixing bowl. Mix in the stevia, Fruitsource, fruit juice, arrowroot powder, cinnamon, vanilla, and salt, coating the peaches. Lay peaches out in bottom of baking pan.

Topping

1 cup w.w. flour
1/4 tsp. salt
1/4 tsp. stevia extract
1/4 tsp. cinnamon
2 tbls. oil
2 tbls. maple syrup

Combine the flour, salt, stevia, and cinnamon in a bowl. Lightly cut in the oil using a fork or your fingers. Rub in the maple syrup until well distributed. Crumble the mixture over the peaches.

Bake for 40-45 minutes. If the top is getting too brown, cover the pan with foil during the last 15-20 minutes of baking.

VARIATION: For part of the flour use wheat germ or ground sesame seeds.

COCONUT BANANA
CREAM PIE

Crust

Prepare a single pie crust. See page 65 or page 68. Prick the bottom and sides with a fork. **Pre-bake the shell at 425° for 10-12 minutes**.

Filling

4 chopped dates
1 1/2 cups soy milk
1/2 cup unsweetened coconut
1 1/3 cups water
1/2 tsp. stevia extract
1 tsp. vanilla extract
3 tbls. arrowroot powder
1 cup tofu whipped cream
1 1/2 tbls. agar-agar (or 1 pkg. gelatin)
2 medium bananas

Grind the chopped dates in a blender with 1/2 cup of the milk until fairly smooth. Add the coconut and 1 cup of water. Grind and process until creamy. Blend in the rest of the milk. Add the stevia, vanilla, and the arrowroot powder and blend. Note: May use a food processor.

Pour the well-blended mixture into a pan and cook while stirring over medium-low heat until thick. Simmer on low heat for 3-5 minutes more, stirring occasionally but gently.

Prepare 1 cup tofu whipped cream (see page 85).

Continued on next page.

Place the agar-agar and 1/3 cup water in a small sauce pan. Bring to a boil, then simmer 3-4 minutes until dissolved. Add the dissolved agar-agar to the tofu whipped cream in the blender and mix. Fold into the pudding.

Layer sliced bananas in the bottom of the cooled pre-baked pie shell. If preferred, half of the bananas may be mashed and folded into the pudding. Pour pudding over bananas in the pie shell.

Dust top of pie with shredded coconut. Chill in the refrigerator at least 2 hours.

NOTE: If you don't have any agar-agar (or gelatin), just use an extra tablespoon or two of arrowroot powder. However, the agar gives a creamier, lighter filling with better shape.

TOPPINGS

AND

SAUCES

BLUEBERRY SAUCE

8 ounces of blueberries (fresh or frozen)
1/2 cup unsweetened apple or grape juice
1/4 tsp. stevia extract
2 tsp. lemon juice
1 tbls. arrowroot powder

Place the berries in a small pan with 1/4 cup juice, the stevia, and lemon juice. Heat until softened.

Process the berries in a blender. Return to the pan and heat on medium-low.

Dissolve the arrowroot powder in the other half of the juice and add to the sauce pan. Heat on low, stirring gently until sauce is thick and shiny. Remove from heat.

NOTE: If using frozen berries, more arrowroot powder may be required.

STRAWBERRY FILLING

1 cup sliced unsweetened strawberries (fresh or frozen)
3/4 cup unsweetened apple juice
1/4 tsp. stevia extract
2 tsp. honey
1 tsp. lemon juice
3 tbls. rice flour
1 tbls. butter or margarine
2 ounces soft tofu

NOTE: If using frozen berries, reduce apple juice to 1/2 cup.

Place the berries and apple juice in a sauce pan and cook a few minutes until soft.

Pour into a blender and process. Return to the pan (keep aside 1/2 cup of the berry sauce). Stir in the stevia, honey, and lemon juice. Heat on medium-low.

Mix the rice flour into the remaining 1/2 cup of sauce. Stir the flour mixture into the hot berry sauce. Bring to a boil, stirring with a wooden spoon until mixture is smooth. Eliminate any lumps. Use a beater if necessary. Remove from heat and beat in the butter (or margarine).

Cream the tofu in a blender. Fold the creamed tofu into the thickened filling.

CREAMY CRANBERRY SAUCE

3 cups fresh cranberries
1 1/2 cups unsweetened apple juice
3 ounces orange juice
2-3 tbls. maple syrup or honey
3/4 tsp. stevia extract
finely grated rind of 1/2 orange

Pick out and discard the soft berries. Place berries in sauce pan with apple juice. Cook over medium heat for 20-30 minutes.

Add the orange juice, maple syrup (or honey), and stevia. Cook over low heat stirring occasionally for 20-30 more minutes.

Add finely grated orange rind and cook 15 to 20 minutes longer, stirring occasionally.

Remove sauce from the heat and put it through a sieve. Results in a thick and smooth sauce.

Yield: about 1 1/2 cups.

VARIATION: For a whole cranberry sauce, place the cranberries, apple juice, stevia, and maple syrup (or honey) in a sauce pan and cook on medium for about 10 minutes (until the skins burst). Add the orange juice and grated peel. Simmer about 5-10 minutes longer until thick.

LEMON ICING

3-4 tbls. rice flour
1 cup water
1/4 tsp. stevia extract
1 tbls. honey
1 tbls. lemon juice
finely grated rind of 1/2 lemon
1 tbls. butter or margarine

In a cup or small bowl, mix the flour into a portion of the water until smooth. Add this flour mixture to the rest of the water in a small sauce pan. Break down any lumps.

Heat on medium stirring continually for several minutes until thick. Reduce heat to low and add the stevia, honey, lemon juice, and rind. Cook a minute more.

Remove from the heat and beat in the butter (or margarine) until smooth and creamy.

Yield: about 1 cup.

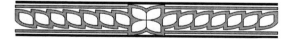

CREAM CHEESE FROSTING

8 ounces soft cream cheese
2 tbls. milk
1 1/2 tbls. lemon juice
finely grated rind of 1/2 lemon
1/4 tsp. stevia
1 tbls. honey

Soften the cream cheese with the milk. Beat in the lemon juice, lemon rind, stevia, and honey. Whip until thoroughly blended and creamy.

Yield: about 1 cup.

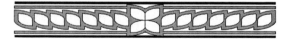

LEMON CREAM

1/2 cup raw cashews
1/2 cup soy milk
2 tbls. lemon juice
finely grated rind of 1/2 lemon
1/4 tsp. stevia (scant)
2 tsp. honey
4 tbls. melted butter or margarine

Grind the cashews and milk together in a blender until smooth. Blend in the lemon juice, rind, stevia, and honey.

Place the mixture in a small mixing bowl. Melt the butter (or margarine) in a small pan. Gradually beat in the melted butter with a hand mixer. Beat on high for about 3 minutes until thick and creamy.

NOTE: May be processed entirely in the blender. Add the melted butter (or margarine) through the center hole of the blender cover.

"WHIPPED CREAM"

1/2 cup raw cashews
1/2 cup soy milk
1/4 tsp. stevia extract
1/2 tsp. vanilla extract
2 tsp. honey, maple syrup, or Fruitsource
pinch of salt
1/2 to 3/4 cup oil

Grind cashews in a blender with the soy milk until creamy using the pulse button. Periodically clean off the sides of the blender. Add the stevia, vanilla, honey, (maple syrup or Fruitsource) and salt. Blend until creamy.

Slowly add the oil in a steady but fine stream through the center hole of the blender cover. Start with 1/2 cup of oil. For a thicker cream add more oil. You should not have to add more than 3/4 cup.

NOTE: A whipped cream can be made using 1/2 cup cashew nuts and 1/2 cup water plus the oil OR simply by using 1/2 cup soy milk plus the oil, but I have found that a thicker cream can be made by combining the cashew nuts with the soy milk. At times, the cream may not get thick enough. It seems to be influenced by the weather.

TOFU "WHIPPED CREAM"

8 ounces soft or silken tofu
2 tbls. oil
1/4 tsp. stevia extract
1 tbls. maple syrup or honey
1/2 tsp. vanilla extract
pinch of salt

Combine all the ingredients in a blender and process until smooth
and creamy.

VARIATIONS: Substitute citrus rind for the vanilla
       OR: Add a few strawberries or other berries.

CASHEW CREAM

1/2 cup raw cashews
1 cup water
1 tbls. oil
1/4 tsp. stevia extract
1 tsp. maple syrup or honey

Grind the cashews in part of the water. Add the rest of the water, the oil, stevia, and maple syrup. Blend until smooth and creamy. Add a little more water if a thinner cream is desired.

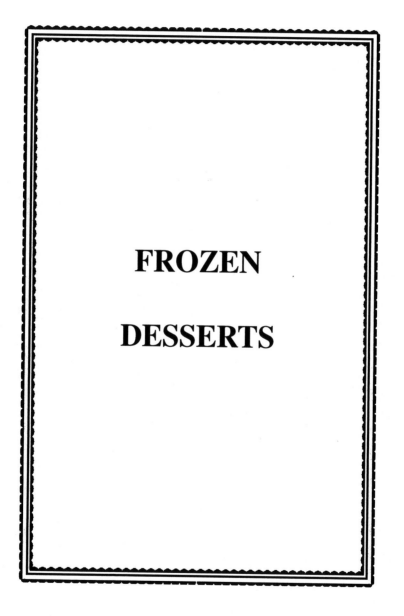

FROZEN

DESSERTS

HOLIDAY CRANBERRY SHERBET

1 1/2 cups cranberry sauce
10 ounces of tofu whipped cream
3 ounces of orange juice from concentrate

Cranberry Sauce

Prepare sauce. Use Creamy Cranberry Sauce recipe (page 80). Chill before using.

Tofu Whipped Cream

10 ounces soft or silken tofu
1/4 tsp. stevia
1 tsp. vanilla
1 tbls. honey

Blend all the ingredients together in a blender until smooth and creamy.

Sherbet

Add the cranberry sauce and orange juice to the tofu whipped cream in the blender. Process until well blended.

Pour into a shallow pan and place in the freezer. Freeze until mushy (about 1 1/2 - 2 hours). Chill a bowl and beaters in the refrigerator.

Remove from freezer and beat with a hand mixer until smooth. Return to pan and freeze hard.

Remove from freezer. Thaw about 15 minutes. Process in a blender, food processor, or hand mixer until smooth. Place sherbet in a closed container and return to freezer. Thaw about 15 minutes before serving.

ORANGE SHERBET

1/2 cup soy whipped cream
3 ounces raw cashews (liquid measure)
1 ounce dried unsweetened coconut (liquid measure)
1 cup orange juice (from concentrate)
1/2 cup papaya or mango juice
1 tsp. lemon juice
1/2 tsp. stevia extract
pinch of salt
1 tbls. agar-agar (or gelatin)
1/2 cup apple juice or water

Prepare the soy whipped cream by blending together 1/4 cup soy milk with 1/4 cup oil, 1/2 tsp. vanilla, and 1 tsp. honey (optional). See page 84. Remove from blender. Set aside. Note: May use dairy whipped cream.

Grind the cashews and coconut in a blender with about 1/2 cup of the orange juice. When creamy, add the rest of the orange juice, papaya or mango juice, lemon juice, stevia, salt, and process.

Place the agar-agar in a small pan with the apple juice and soak for 1 minute. Simmer on low heat for about 3 minutes until dissolved. Mix the agar-agar into the blender ingredients.

Fold or blend the soy whipped cream into the blender ingredients. Pour into a shallow pan and place in the freezer. Chill a bowl and beaters. When consolidated but still mushy (about 1 1/2 to 2 hours) remove from the freezer and beat with a hand mixer until smooth. Return to the pan and refreeze.

When frozen hard remove from the freezer and soften about 15 minutes. Process the sherbet in a blender, food processor, or hand mixer until creamy with a fine grain. Spoon into a covered container and return to the freezer.

"There are so many plants on the planet that are given to us to use to be healthy, and I believe stevia is one of those plants."

Donna Gates - Author of *The Body Ecology Diet* and co-author of *The Stevia Story*

"The fact is that the sweetening power of Kaá hè-é (stevia) is so superior to sugar that there is no need to wait for the results of analyses and cultures to affirm its economic advantage."

Moisés S. Bertoni - Italian botanist introduced to the plant by indigenous people of Paraguay. From a description of the plant published in 1905.

❖ RESOURCES ❖

INSTRUCTIVE COOKBOOKS

The American Vegetarian Cookbook from the Fit for Life Kitchen by Marilyn Diamond

The *Ten Talents* Cookbook by Frank and Rosalie Hurd

The New Laurel's Kitchen by Laurel Robertson, Carol Flinders and Brian Ruppenthal

The Joy of Cooking by Irma Rombauer and Marion Rombauer Becker

Great Cakes by Carole Walter

Tofu Cookery by Louise Hagler

BAKING EQUIPMENT SOURCES

Williams-Sonoma Company   San Francisco, CA
1-800-541-1262   Free catalog

Bridge Kitchenware   New York, NY
1-212-688-4220   Catalog $3

Sweet Celebrations   Minneapolis, MN
1-800-328-6722   Free catalog

BOOKS ABOUT STEVIA

The Stevia Story by Linda Bonvie, Bill Bonvie & Donna Gates
The history, politics and uses of stevia, with recipes.

Stevia: Nature's Sweet Secret by David Richard
Information and recipes.

MAKING LIQUID
STEVIA EXTRACT

Bring 2 cups of purified water to a boil. Reduce heat to medium and add 1/4 cup of crushed or powdered dried stevia leaves. Cover and boil for 3 minutes. Remove from the heat and steep the herb in a covered pot until cool. Strain through a cheesecloth and refrigerate in a covered container. **The concentrate will be dark greenish black in color.**

5 drops	=	2 tbls. sugar
20 drops	=	1 /2 cup sugar
3/4 tsp.	=	1 cup sugar

For a **cold extraction** soak 1/4 cup of the powdered leaf in 2 cups of water for 8-12 hours on the counter. Strain through a cheesecloth.

For a stronger concentrate, simmer the liquid (from either method above) uncovered on the stove until it is reduced by half. Refrigerate.

Note: A white powdered extract was used for the recipes in this book. This green liquid extraction may also be used. See the equivalencies on page 4.

Further Information Available

For Free Information
on all stevia powders and liquids call:
1-800-899-9908
or visit
www.wisdomherbs.com and **www.steviaplus.com**.

Stevia Products available from
Wisdom of the Ancients®
and the
SweetLeaf ™ Company include:

SteviaPlus™
Stevia Clear™
Stevia Extract Powder
Stevia Concentrate
HoneyLeaf™ Brand Ground Stevia Leaf
HoneyLeaf™ Brand Stevia Leaf Tea Bags

Wisdom of the Ancients®, makers of the SweetLeaf™ Brand, is the worldwide leading supplier of stevia and other medicinal herbs of Paraguay.

Made By

QUALITY YOU CAN TASTE

ABOUT THE AUTHOR

Rita DePuydt is a botanist and a free-lance writer/photographer, originally from Michigan, now living in California. She also has a background in Home-Economics and as a Medical Laboratory Technician.

Health and healing herbs have been an interest of hers for several decades. She was a leader in a nutrition education and activist group during her college years, was on the education committee of her local food coop for several years, and has taught whole food cooking classes.

Rita has been dealing with sugar sensitivity since a child. Following numerous ups and downs, she became interested in stevia as a way of reducing her consumption of sugars and is experimenting with the herb to discover if it helps balance her blood sugar levels and reduce sugar cravings.